Ma

Dan Colwell

JPMGUIDES

Contents

- **This Way Maldives** 3
- **Flashback** 7
- **On the Scene** 15
  - *Male* 15
  - *Kaafu* 27
  - *Other Resorts* 39
- **Cultural Notes** 50
- **Shopping** 52
- **Sports** 53
- **Dining Out** 54
- **The Hard Facts** 56
- *Index* 64

Maps
  The Maldives 6

Fold-out map
  Male
  North Male Atoll
  South Male Atoll
  Lhaviyani Atoll
  Baa Atoll
  Ari Atoll
  Northern Maldives
  Southern Maldives
  Felidhoo Atoll
  Addu Atoll

This Way Maldives

Island Nation

Anyone who has ever dreamed of escaping to a tropical island basking in year-round sunshine, surrounded by sparkling white, palm-fringed beaches and turquoise seas will find that the real thing exists in abundance in the Maldives. For this chain of more than 1000 coral islands strung out across the Indian Ocean consists entirely of serious contenders for the title of paradise.

The first—and best—view that most visitors get is from the air as they approach the capital, Male. The islands are arranged in clusters of atolls, a word that the Maldivian language has given to English. Heart-shaped, circular, oblong, they appear as spectacular explosions of green, turquoise and aquamarine in the dark-blue waters of the deep ocean.

Up close, you realise that the islands are little more than palm-covered sandbanks. The Republic of Maldives, to use its formal name, is one of the lowest-lying countries on earth. The highest peak in the land is but 2 m (6.5 ft) above sea level, and it is only the presence of barrier reefs surrounding the atolls that prevents the Maldives from disappearing beneath the waves.

It might seem remarkable that they exist at all, given their isolated setting in the vast ocean. In fact, each island is a coral-encrusted summit of a range of submerged volcanoes stretching from just off the Indian sub-continent to south of the equator. It's an intriguing thought that as you lie on the beach soaking up the sun, you are actually perched on top of a huge mountain. You will soon discover that there's often more to the island nation than appears on its tranquil surface.

People of the Sea

Perhaps it's not surprising that in a country where more than 99.5% of the territory is water, the sea plays a pivotal role in the lives of the inhabitants. This is truly a nation of boatmen, and whether their distinctive traditional Maldivian craft—called *dhonis*—are being used to navigate the treacherous reefs as water-taxis or for all-important daily fishing expeditions, Maldivians have long been renowned for their nautical skills.

A population of 339,000 is scattered across 200 of the islands, but has nonetheless remained surprisingly close-knit. The Maldivian people share a

THIS WAY MALDIVES

highly individual and homogeneous culture, cemented together by a common language, Dhivehi, and a common religion, Islam: every citizen of the Maldives is a Muslim.

One thing that impresses visitors is the genuine friendliness and courtesy of the islanders. Although they are as peaceable a people as you are ever likely to find, Maldivians remain fiercely independent. Their idyllic country may have been coveted by many larger nations over the centuries, but they take particular pride in being able to boast that the Maldives has only once been occupied by a foreign power in all its history, and that for a mere 15 years during the 16th century.

A First Resort

Tourism began in the Maldives as recently as 1972, when two fairly basic resorts were opened at Kurumba and Bandos Island. In those days it was mainly a side-trip for people staying in Sri Lanka. Times have changed, and people now head directly for the very obvious charms of the Maldives. There are over 90 resorts now, with more planned. Constant upgrading makes a stay at any one of them never less than a lesson in relaxation.

Once you are comfortably ensconced in your resort, you may find it difficult to leave again—literally. Each one is self-contained on its own "uninhabited" island—that is, no Maldivians live on them—and, apart from organized island-hopping, there is no independent ferry service for you to escape on. But lucky Robinson Crusoes usually see little reason to try. The restaurants are always bountiful, the sun shines on average for eight hours every day of the year, and the ocean is famous the world over for the wondrous underwater sights within easy reach of every resort.

Island Capital

Male is the economic and political hub of this far-flung country, and its 75,000 inhabitants are

---

1 THE MOST REMOTE ATOLL Foreigners are mainly restricted to resort islands in the atolls near Male and require a permit to visit inhabited islands. But for a unique experience of life in the Maldives, fly 500 km (300 miles) south to Gan in **Addu Atoll**, where you will be free to walk around Maldivian fishing villages and mix with the islanders.

THIS WAY MALDIVES

Every evening, nature provides a glorious sunset.

crammed onto an island of a mere 1.5 sq km (about half a square mile). Here, in vivid contrast to the unbroken calm of most other parts of the Maldives, is all the hustle and bustle of a lively tropical city, with noisy markets, busy traffic and a dramatic waterfront crowded with rows of fishing boats unloading their catch, trading ships and sea-taxis. Meanwhile, residents, shopkeepers and workers merge with sightseeing day-trippers flocking in from the resort islands.

Male has been the nation's centre of power for more than 800 years, but has only recently undergone a population explosion. The island capital has been obliged to expand physically in order to accommodate its growing importance. More than a third of today's city is built on land reclaimed from the sea.

Small wonder, then, that Male increasingly has the atmosphere of a boom town. Newer and higher buildings are going up, despite all good intentions that nothing should be taller than the minaret of the Grand Friday Mosque. Traditionalists may deplore it, but as the view from any approaching *dhoni* will confirm, the Male skyline is shaping up to be the region's own mini-Manhattan.

Flashback

First Inhabitants

No one really knows when the first settlers arrived in the Maldives, nor where they came from. However, it is likely that they sailed over from the nearest landmasses, India and Sri Lanka, no later than the 5th century BC. During the 1920s, excavations of pre-Islamic *hawittas,* or coral mounds, on the outlying atolls revealed a wealth of Buddhist artefacts, suggesting a predominantly Sri Lankan influence. There were some Hindu relics as well, which may point to an early Maldivian ability to embrace a mix of foreign cultures.

A unique Maldivian language and culture evolved, as well as a set of myths and legends about the magical nature of the islands. These centred mainly on the *jinni*—supernatural beings who control and affect the actions of humans both for good and evil. Despite the subsequent advent of Islam, a belief in the *jinni,* and the use of charms and spells to combat them, continues to this day.

Ocean Hub

The Maldives lie bang in the middle of one of the world's oldest and greatest trade routes, between Arabia, East Africa, India and the Far East, and over the centuries, a cosmopolitan assortment of traders passed this way. They had to negotiate the notoriously dangerous reefs, which were feared by seafarers from around the world. Indeed, 2nd-century Greek geographers thought the islands were magnetic and attracted ships to destruction on their rocks.

The Arab traders noted two things in particular: the forwardness of Maldivian women, many of whom became wives to Arabian sailors for the duration of their stay, and the huge amounts of cowries—small seashells that were used as currency. In fact, for many years the Maldives were known as the Cowrie Isles.

Arrival of Islam

Although contact with Arabia was longstanding, it was not until 1153 that the Maldives adopted Islam as its religion. It was accomplished through conversion rather than conquest, however, and true to form a colourful story surrounds the event. According to legend, the incumbent Buddhist king was plagued by a troublesome sea *jinni* called Rannamaari, who demanded the sacrifice of a virgin each full moon. An Arab trader named Abu al

▶ FLASHBACK

Barakaath heard of this and offered to help. He managed to cast out the *jinni* by taking the place of the young woman and, as Rannamaari approached, recited the Holy Koran out loud. The *jinni* fled, never to return, and the king, suitably impressed, decided to convert to Islam.

A more prosaic explanation argues that the real reason for the conversion was simply that the small nation wished to remain independent. Fear of their closest neighbour, Buddhist Sri Lanka, meant that the Maldives' rulers hoped to secure the backing of their powerful Arabic allies, something best guaranteed by sharing the same religion. Whichever interpretation is preferred, the Maldivian king changed his title to Sultan Mohamed Ibn Abdulla and established the first in a series of Islamic sultanates that transformed the country and would last for the next 800 years.

Portuguese Occupation

In the centuries after the advent of Islam, the Maldives continued along its mainly peaceful path, charming visitors, trading with its neighbours, even seeing women reach the top job as Sultana. However, the 16th century was to prove one of the most tumultuous in Maldivian history. Following Vasco da Gama's celebrated voyage to Cochin, southwest India, in 1498, the Portuguese became the dominant power in the region. By 1518 they had established a foothold in Male, building a fort to protect their trading interests. Finally, in 1558, they launched a full-scale invasion under Captain Andreas Andre. The ruling Sultan Ali VI was killed and Andre proclaimed himself Sultan. The 15 years of Portuguese rule, the only period in their history that the Maldives have been governed by a foreign power, were probably the cruellest the islanders have suffered. Andre took it upon himself to convert the population to Christianity with a policy of conversion or death, and the subsequent resistance saw a considerable amount of bloodshed throughout the islands.

2 **THE TWO BEST FESTIVALS** Steam is always let off in great quantities during **Kuda Eid**, a time of feasting and merriment celebrating the end of the month-long fasting period of Ramadan. The **Republic Day** festival in November sees parades and marching bands take over the capital.

FLASHBACK

The Maldivians never gave in to their occupiers, and the Portuguese faced years of guerrilla warfare. The fragmented nature of the country made it extremely difficult to conquer completely, and it was on one of the outlying northern islands, Utheemu, that a new leader emerged. In 1573, Mohamed Thakurufaanu, the son of a local chief, and his Maldivian rebels made a secret night-time landing in Male. The Portuguese garrison was caught totally by surprise and massacred. Further attempts at reinstating Portuguese authority were made, but their power in the Maldives was irretrievably broken.

To the victor the spoils. Not only did the triumphant Thakurufaanu become the new Sultan, setting up the Utheemu dynasty which would rule for more than 130 years, but he has remained the Maldives' most celebrated national hero.

Necessary Diplomacy

In order to achieve his victory, Thakurufaanu had needed to enlist the help of the Malabars from southern India. One of the unexpected repercussions was that with the decline of Portuguese interests in the Maldives, the Malabars considered themselves next in line to take control of the archipelago. Malabar attacks on Male were to occur sporadically —and unsuccessfully—throughout the 17th and 18th centuries, provoking what must be the only offensive launched by a Maldivian army on foreign soil. One of Thakurufaanu's descendants, Sultan Ibrahim Iskandar I, who reigned 1648–87, ordered an invasion of Malabar territory, and the subsequent capture of some local bigwigs gained him a large ransom and peace for the rest of his reign.

BODU BERU

The best-known traditional Maldivian dance is an uncharacteristically raucous event, possibly because it provides a sanctioned way for the people of this self-controlled society to let their hair down. *Bodu beru* refers to the large drum, made from a hollowed-out piece of coconut tree and the dried skin of a stingray, that hammers out the hypnotic beat of the dance. At least three drummers and fifteen dancers—all male—take part, building up from slow, monotonous movements to a frantic climax in which some of the dancers might end in a trance. The rhythmic music reflects its African origins; *bodu beru* found its way to the Maldives with the many sailors who came here from East Africa, and settled.

FLASHBACK

This period saw the consolidation of the Maldives' relations with the new dominant European power. The Dutch had conquered Sri Lanka, and the Maldivians signed a treaty with the Dutch governor there in 1645. It was typical of Maldivian diplomatic strategy that Holland's status was essentially that of protector, allowing the Maldives full political autonomy.

British Protectorate

The Maldives has always been profoundly affected by events in Sri Lanka. When, in 1796, the British wrested control of the country from the Dutch, they also assumed the protectorship of its island neighbour. One positive result was the extensive survey of the Maldives in 1834 by a Royal Navy Commander, Robert Moresby, whose charts are still in use today.

Trade between Male and Colombo was boosted at first, but by the middle of the 19th century the Maldivian economy was in bad shape. Most of the trade had become monopolized by Borah merchants from Bombay, and local resentment was such that by 1887 civil unrest began to destabilize the capital. In order to gain leverage with the merchants and re-establish order, Sultan Mohamed Muinuddin II signed a treaty with Britain, by now the greatest power in the Indian Ocean, and the Maldives formally became a British Protectorate. The most important issue at stake for the Sultan, however, was to legally bind the British to keep out of the Maldives' domestic affairs. Once again, canny Maldivian diplomacy had secured the country's fundamental independence.

Early 20th Century

A movement towards greater democracy in the first part of the century led to Sultan Shamsuddeen III having to accept the nation's first written constitution in 1932. This curtailed the powers of the sultan and paved the way for elections. Ultimately, its effect was to weaken the position of the sultan to the extent that the title became obsolete.

World War II brought some economic revival when renewed interest in the Maldives' strategic location meant that the British built two new airstrips on islands at either end of the country. The loss of Britain's colony in Sri Lanka in 1948 only boosted their importance, as the Maldives became Britain's last foothold in the region. A defence pact that year strengthened Britain's control of Maldivian foreign policy.

Bashful schoolgirl on Bodufolodhu. Every Maldivian is a Muslim.

As the power of the sultan withered, so the prestige of the prime minister flourished. By the 1950s, prime minister Mohamed Amin Didi was almost in complete control and put through a package of reforms, including the nationalization of the fish export industry. It was a short step from here to abolishing the sultanate and proclaiming a republic. Amin Didi became the Maldives' first president in 1953. Food shortages and a reckless attempt to impose a ban on tobacco smoking meant he was driven from office within a year. In his wake, the sultanate was restored, with Mohamed Farid Didi (no relation) being elected the 94th—and final, as it turned out—sultan of the Maldives.

Regaining Sovereignty

In 1956, the British negotiated a 100-year lease on the air base they had built on the island of Gan, in the southernmost atoll, during World War II. When prime minister Ibrahim Nasir came to power the following year, he revoked the lease, demanding a shorter term and higher rent. The inhabitants of the southern atolls, who had benefited from the income and employment that the British air base created, were resentful of the government in Male, and in 1959 they broke away from the Maldives to form the United Suvadive Islands, with their own prime minister. Nasir proved too wily a politician to allow this to continue, and by 1962 he had succeeded in agreeing terms with the British and, backed by gun-

---

A HISTORY OF TOURISM

Although tourism officially began in the Maldives in 1972, travellers have been delighted by the place for more than a thousand years. The most famous was Marco Polo, who summed it up in the 14th century as the "flower of the Indies". The early Indians who came here obviously agreed and thought of the archipelago as a beautiful chain of flowers —the name 'Maldives' comes from the Sanskrit word for "garland of islands". Ibn Battuta, an Arab trader, landed here in 1344 and stayed for 10 months. By the time he left he had acquired two wives, a high-ranking position in Maldivian society and the opinion that this was "one of the wonders of the world". In these modern times, a stream of visitors has confirmed Battuta's view. Now 467,000 people come to the Maldives each year—more than there are inhabitants of these delightful islands.

FLASHBACK

boats from Male, routing the renegades in the south and reuniting the country.

Britain granted total independence to the Maldives only three years later, although the RAF base on Gan remained in operation until 1976. Nasir's prestige was such that, in a 1968 referendum, the people voted to end the sultanate once again and establish a second republic, with the prime minister raised to the position of president. The tiny nation joined the United Nations as a fully independent sovereign state member in 1975.

The Maldives Today

The powers of the president were significantly increased in a 1972 amendment to the constitution, and fairly soon Maldivians began to accuse Nasir of authoritarianism and corruption. The market for the islands' biggest export, tuna, collapsed in 1972. The advent of the tourist industry in the Maldives the same year did nothing to help Nasir's reputation, as he was said to have used public funds to start his own hotel business. Finally, in 1978, Nasir fled to Singapore with a large quantity of the nation's cash in his suitcase.

His successor, Maumoon Abdul Gayoom, has been a necessary antidote, a model of propriety and a believer in more open government. With his encouragement, tourism has become a carefully managed money-spinner for the country, and the revenue has been used to aid education and health. Nevertheless, he has had to survive three coup attempts, the last one in 1988 when local businessmen hired Sri Lankan Tamil mercenaries to stage an overthrow. Gayoom won the day by calling on the Indian government for assistance, the most recent example in a long history of Maldivian readiness to employ larger allies without compromising political independence.

The Maldivian economy has expanded greatly since Gayoom came to power, though the country is still one of the least developed on earth. The problem facing him and his nation remains how to sustain growth without upsetting the unique culture and environment of the Maldives. Male is beset by severe overcrowding, while the influence of tourism has so far been kept separate from traditional indigenous fishing communities.

In the long term, Gayoom has identified a danger that makes everything else potentially irrelevant. Any rise in the sea level would be a catastrophe. The effects of global in the 21st century might see the Maldives, in the President's words, "disappear from the earth".

On the Scene

There are 26 natural atolls in the Maldives, divided into 20 administrative areas. The majority are only accessible to tourists with an inter-atoll permit, issued by the Ministry of Atolls Administration in Male. The resort islands are mainly located in the atolls closest to Male—the North and South Male Atolls and Ari Atoll—with the notable exception of Gan in Addu Atoll in the extreme south of the country. The resorts enjoy varying degrees of comfort, but diving and snorkelling facilities are almost universally available, and many also boast tennis courts and fully equipped gyms. Day trips are usually available to a representative Maldivian village on an inhabited island.

MALE
The City, Around Male

No matter which resort island you choose for your stay, don't miss the chance of an expedition to Male. This delightful tropical capital offers the chance to experience Maldivian culture in its own environment.

When the English archaeologist H.C.P. Bell visited Male in the 1920s, he described a city teeming with 5,000 inhabitants and complained that it was far too overcrowded. Today, 75,000 people—a quarter of the entire nation—live here, and the figure is constantly rising. This is the location of the main hospitals, and the schools of higher education. It's also the seat of government and the civil service, home to the security services and the centre of trade and business. To Maldivians, it's the place of opportunity and advancement, and many who come here from the islands never leave again.

Somehow, despite the traffic and the crowds, the city manages to retain the character of a charm-

A flurry of activity down by the commercial harbour, where all manner of goods are unloaded.

THE CITY

ing little town as well as a busy capital. There's not a sight or a shop that's more than a short walk away, and the streets remain safe to stroll around by day or night. The intimate tea houses and cafés are great places for striking up conversations with the islanders. And sitting out on the Jumhooree Maidhan, the main square, enjoying the breeze as the sun sets and the muezzin calls from the minaret of the Grand Friday Mosque, is an experience that sets you in a different world.

The City

It's not too difficult to find your way around the city, even though its narrow side-streets can seem dauntingly labyrinthine. The main points of interest are all contained on the north part of the island within the perimeter of two long roads, Marine Drive (now officially known by the tongue-twisting Boduthakurufaanu Ma-

gu), which curves around the harbourfront, and Majeedi Magu, running straight as a die across the middle of the island. There are no beaches; Male is surrounded by sea walls on all sides. The southern part has been reclaimed from the sea.

Most of the boats from the resort islands land near Jumhooree Maidhan, a good starting point for a walking tour.

Jumhooree Maidhan

The layout of this large public square was completed only in 1989, when the lawns and trees were planted and benches installed, but it is now very much the beating heart of the capital, a meeting place and hang-out for young and old alike. The Maidhan is dominated by a tall flagpole with an impressively vast Maldivian flag.

If you stand in the centre of the square looking out to sea, the

3 **THE THREE BEST MOSQUES Hukuru Miskiiy**, in Male, was built in the mid-17th century during the reign of the charismatic Sultan Ibrahim Iskandar I. The great gold-coloured dome of the capital's splendid **Grand Friday Mosque** dominates the city skyline and can be seen from far out at sea. **Aasaari Miskiiy** on Nilandhoo in the North Nilandhoo Atoll can claim its origins way back in the 12th century, during the reign of the first sultan to convert the Maldives to Islam.

THE CITY

fancy wooden structure in front of you is the President's Jetty, used only for grand arrivals in Male by the president and visiting foreign dignitaries.

Face the other direction and you will see the high, white-washed walls of the National Security Service building. Signs tell you not to take photographs and, with its watchtowers constantly manned, it's wise to take heed. This building bore the brunt of the 1988 coup attempt, and it is probably the only place in the Maldives where any nervousness on the part of the military is at all visible.

Islamic Centre and Grand Friday Mosque

The Islamic Centre, incorporating the Sultan Mohamed Thakuru-faanu Mosque, to call it by its official name, is without question Male's most outstanding architectural flourish. The beautifully proportioned golden dome of the mosque, made from treated aluminium, gives the city skyline a distinction it might otherwise lack, and the sun's glistening reflection on it can be seen from as far as Bandos Island, 10 km (6 miles) away. Rows of arched windows cut a stylistic dash on the building's white exterior. The slim, three-tiered minaret, from which the muezzin calls worshippers to prayer, sports jagged grey

and white chevrons and is topped with a matching gold dome.

Reached from a pathway situated just behind Jumhooree Maidhan, it is the Maldives' principal mosque, and can hold up to 5,000 worshippers at a time. The first-floor gallery allows a view of the splendid interior, decorated with finely carved wooden panels and elegant Arabic calligraphy. The mosque is closed to visitors during prayertime. Don't forget

---

A QUESTION OF ACCENT

One controversy in Male has nothing to do with politics or economics but is the long-standing problem of how its name should be written. The word is pronounced *Mar-lay*, and you will often see it written with a trailing apostrophe (Male') which is said, by some, to have come about because the old British typewriters that were used weren't equipped with an acute accent to go over the last letter. It creates havoc when you want to use the possessive form! Younger radicals now favour Malé, while others have sought to usher in a less formal era by dropping any kind of diacritical mark. In an attempt to keep things simple, we have preferred here to adopt this last solution.

▶ THE CITY

to remove your shoes before entering.

The Islamic Centre was officially opened on Republic Day in November 1984, a symbolic moment to demonstrate how far the country had come in only two decades. More than a place of worship, it's an affirmation of the centrality of Islamic culture in the Maldives, and as such contains a library, schoolrooms and a meeting hall as well.

Sultan Park

The great iron gates of this small and very pleasant tropical park just a short distance from the Islamic Centre were once the entrance to the sultan's palace. The park itself was created out of the palace grounds after the palace was destroyed in 1968 following the establishment of the Second Republic. It is a lovingly tended oasis of calm in the bustle of the modern capital, with lily ponds, exotic plants, and palm and banyan trees giving plenty of shade. Photographers will also find some good angles on the Grand Friday Mosque from here.

National Museum

The three-storey building inside the park is the only surviving remnant of the sultan's palace and now houses the National Museum. It has a highly eclectic group of exhibits, and despite the sometimes eccentric layout it provides an interesting glimpse into

---

SURPRISING SULTANAS

Women have a long history of achieving political power in countries around this part of the Indian Ocean, and those in the Maldives are no exception. Two of the most remarkable—and ruthless—were the Sultana Khadeeja Kileji, who reigned on and off for 38 years until her death in 1380 and dispatched a brother and two husbands in order to gain the throne; and Mariam Kabaafaanu, who began as a slave girl but became the mistress of Sultan Ibrahim Iskandar. Their son inherited the title in 1687, but Mariam seized power herself. She not only enjoyed a string of lovers but encouraged the women of her court to do the same. Her death came when, sailing out to meet a Maldivian fleet which had defeated the Malabars, a stray spark from a victory cannonade set off her boat's store of gunpowder and blew it to smithereens. There have been no recent Sultanas in the Maldives, but tradition suggests that it may only be a matter of time before the first female president heads the country.

THE CITY

Maldivian history. The bulk of the collection focuses on the lives of the sultans over the last few centuries, ranging from threadbare thrones, luxurious palanquins and sedan chairs to embroidered coats, sultanate umbrellas and other minutiae of royal life.

Alongside these is a remarkable jumble of items including four pieces of moonrock and a small Maldivian flag taken on the first manned flight to the moon in 1969; some beautiful examples of traditional Maldivian lacquerware; a couple of bullet-riddled motorbikes from the 1988 coup attempt; and a weapons room with muskets, swords and *bonthi*, large sticks used in martial arts. There's a good display of stamps, banknotes and coins, including unusual 17th-century ones that look like hairgrips. But the most important displays are the intriguing archaeological finds brought here from temples uncovered on the outer islands, such as a pre-Islamic Buddha's head carved in coral and sandstone. Surprisingly, this sits among the bric-a-brac on the veranda outside the entrance.

Hukuru Miskiiy

Turn right at the park gates and head east along Medhuziyaarai Magu. On the left is the Maldives' oldest and most attractive mosque, although its corrugated iron roof (protecting the coral stone from sunlight) looks unflattering at first sight. Built in 1656 by Sultan Ibrahim Iskandar I, the mosque itself is altogether a different matter. The outside walls made from coral are intricately ornamented with carvings and Arabic script, while the dark interior has richly worked wooden panels, doorways and ceilings.

Non-Muslims are allowed access inside the mosque with permission from the Ministry of Justice and Islamic Affairs. They are otherwise free to walk around the grounds which contain an ancient graveyard with some superbly carved headstones and larger graves, including those of former sultans. Stones with round tops mark women's graves, those with pointed tops are men's.

The squat blue and white hooped tower that sits by the roadside is the *munnaaru*, or minaret. Until 1984, when the Grand Friday Mosque took over its rôle, this was where the chief muezzin of Male would call from at prayertime. It looks like a modern addition to the mosque, but in fact dates from 1675 and was modelled on minarets seen by Sultan Iskandar on his pilgrimage to Mecca.

Mulee-aage

On the opposite side of the road, this modest but colourful palace was built in a Sri Lankan-influ-

19

THE CITY

enced colonial style for Sultan Shamsuddeen III's son in the early 20th century, although it has never had a royal resident. The sultan was deposed before its completion and it was used for administrative offices instead. During the first short-lived republic in 1953 its status rose again when it became the President's Palace, but the current president moved to a new building in 1994.

WHAT'S IN A NAME?

However exotic the streets in Male might seem to foreigners, a closer look at the plaques outside many of the buildings reveals something incongruously familiar, like finding yourself transplanted in an equatorial English village. House names such as Blue Bell, Snow Down and Gold Flint evoke bucolic or cosy images of more northerly climes, while the Seagull Café might just as easily be located in a town on the English Channel. The reason is that the only lasting affect more than a century of British influence has had on the Maldives is a relish for the English language. Such enthusiasm occasionally gives an unintended impression—the seedy-sounding Queen of the Night is in fact one of Male's best waterfront tea houses.

Medhu Ziyaaraiy

Immediately next to the Muleeaage is the striking blue and white façade of the shrine dedicated to Abu al Barakaath, the man credited with bringing Islam to the Maldives in 1153.

Majeedi Magu

Continue along Medhuziyaarai Magu, past the People's Majlis (the new parliament building), and turn right onto Sosun Magu, which leads to Majeedi Magu. This long road, the Oxford Street of Male, bisects the island and is packed with shops and cafés. It gets particularly lively after sundown. The National Stadium, where all the nation's main sporting events take place, is on the left as you head west. Halfway down on the other side, the National Library receives English newspapers and also has books in English, including some on the Maldives.

Tomb of Mohamed Thakurufaanu

A small turning to the right just after the National Library takes you into the quiet backstreets of the capital. Carry on to the small Bihuroazu Kamanaa Mosque on the corner of Neelafaru Magu, where the tomb of the Maldives' great national hero and scourge of the Portuguese sits unobtrusively within its compound.

THE CITY

Singapore Bazaar

Navigate a couple more side-streets west from the tomb and you come to the main post office on Chandani Magu. This road runs all the way back to the waterfront, passing the Islamic Centre and Sultan Park on the right, but before you get there you arrive at a tangle of lively shopping streets known informally as the Singapore Bazaar. The area centres on the top part of Chandani, Fareedhee, Orchid and Faamudheyri streets. There's a profusion of souvenir shops here, as well as some of the capital's better restaurants and tea houses. On Fareedhee Magu, the excellent Novelty Bookshop has good value posters, cards and books which it prints itself in Male.

Theemuge

Located on Orchid Magu, the new Presidential Palace is an attractive blue and white architectural confection that's been home to the president since 1994. The walls are guarded by watchtowers and, as with the National Security Service building in the main square, be careful where you point your camera.

Local Market

Follow the road left of the Theemuge to the harbour, where the capital's markets are to be found. At the back of the President's Palace, the fruit and vegetable market is filled with stalls selling mainly bananas, coconuts, betel leaf and bottles of *dhiyaa hakuru,* a honey-like syrup tapped from palm trees.

In front is an open space where the inhabitants of outlying atolls come to sell firewood or other goods, while in a building next door you can buy smoked or dried fish.

Fish Market

One of the best sights in the city lies along the waterfront, back towards Jumhooree Maidhan. The fish market has an atmosphere as rich as its aroma, and the product for sale on its slithery tiles is a central feature of Maldivian life. The best time to arrive is after 3 p.m., when the fishing *dhonis* fill the harbour and the day's catch of tuna, bonito and swordfish are rushed into the market to be expertly gutted and cleaned. Prices are vigorously haggled over, and buyers for hotels or simply that evening's family supper can be seen heading off on mopeds or pushbikes clutching handfuls of fat fish by the tail.

To add to the flavour, the Fishmarket Café is probably as raucous as any bar ever gets in Male, although you won't find any alcohol there. No Maldivian women either—the rowdy rituals of the

▶ THE CITY

fish market are very much a male preserve that few local women would even dream of attending.

Waterfront

A delightful way to end a walk around the capital is to take in the sunset and enjoy the refreshing breezes on Marine Drive. Apart from the fishing boats, other trading vessels can be seen unloading all manner of produce in the Commercial Harbour west of the fish market, overseen by the impressive ship-like Port Authority building. The waterfront here is lined by old godowns, or warehouses.

Facing out to sea at various points along the waterfront are several ancient cannon. They date mainly from the 17th century and were purchased from the Dutch colony on Sumatra. Aimed at potential Portuguese and Malabar invaders, they were located on a wall 2.5 m (8 ft) high that once surrounded the city. These fortifications lasted until the 1960s when, sadly, they were demolished due to the need for land reclamation. The cannon were tipped into the sea where they came in handy for many years as moorings for *dhonis*. Some have since been dredged up and restored, and now they adorn scenic waterfront locations such as the President's Jetty.

Around Male

Just a glance at the ocean surrounding the capital tells you that this is a busy shipping channel, and not necessarily the most scenic part of the country, even if it is probably the most interesting, and where most of the action is. The water, inevitably, isn't great for swimming, although divers will find one of the country's best known shipwrecks, the 83-m (272-ft) *Maldive Victory*, which sank just off Hulhule in 1981.

MAGICAL AIRPORT

Although it shows few signs of it now, Hulhule Island, on which Male International Airport stands, was once one of two mysterious, thickly wooded islands. It had a sinister reputation among the people of Male and was believed to possess a resident *jinni*, known for her great beauty and ability to captivate unsuspecting men from the capital. Nothing more seems to have been heard of her since the runway was completed in 1968, linking up Hulhule with its neighbour and seeing the last of its inhabitants moved off the island. No doubt the noise levels of the regular influx of jet airliners persuaded the *jinni* to look for a new home as well.

AROUND MALE

The gold-domed Grand Friday Mosque and Islamic Centre are Male's most distinctive buildings.

Funadhoo

Nowadays, the oil storage tanks on Funadhoo blot the view northeast from Male, but the island has had a colourful past. The brother of Mohamed Thakurufaanu was killed by the Portuguese and his head brought to the governor as a trophy. Stolen back by the Maldivians, it was buried here in secret.

Dhoonidhoo

The British governor, based here until 1964, had his residence on Dhoonidhoo, just to the north. The island now has a recent phenomenon in the Maldives—a jailhouse, which is used mainly for political prisoners.

Viligili

West of the capital, this was used as a resort island until 1990, and foreigners are still allowed access. To reach it, take a *dhoni* from Male. There are longstanding plans to use Viligili as an overspill suburb, though they have not met with much success so far as it seems that people are reluctant to move away from the main city.

The island has a decent beach on the east side that affords an excellent view of Male's outer harbour, where the big trading ships have to drop anchor and unload their cargo onto *dhonis* for transport to the wharves.

1. *Blue-headed angel fish*
2. *Coral grouper*
3. *Coachman*
4. *Lion fish*
5. *Clown fish*
6. *Surgeon fish*

KAAFU
North Male Atoll, South Male Atoll

For administrative purposes, the 106 islands of North and South Male Atolls come under the legislation of the Kaafu district. The capital island is is Thulusdhoo, where new fibreglass *dhonis* are built, and the nation's supply of Coca-Cola is concocted with water from the desalination plant. Thulusdhoo is also famous for the manufacture of *bodu beru* drums (see p. 9) and performances of the traditional dance they accompany.

North Male Atoll
In many ways, North Male Atoll is the bedrock of tourism in the Maldives. It was here that the first resorts were opened in 1972, and the atoll now has more than a third of the country's resort islands. Their popularity stems from the proximity to both the airport and Male—which can be a boon for those who feel the need to escape from their island for a shopping and sightseeing break in the city—while still managing to retain an atmosphere of blissful seclusion. Conversely, some of the islands are enlivened by visits from expats who live in Male and fancy the twin luxuries of a sandy beach and a licensed bar.

Kurumba Village
When it opened on Vihamanaa Island in 1972, Kurumba Village ushered in a brave new world of international tourism for the remote island nation. It has metamorphosed into a luxury hotel, with excellent restaurants and bars, a first-class swimming pool, floodlit tennis courts, sports centre and diving school. The island is close to Male and the airport, although generally the noise of the aircraft is unobtrusive.

Farukolhufushi
Club Med is based on the island, and runs the all-in accommodation, meals and activities package which has made the operator so successful in Europe. The main hotel complex was destroyed by fire in 1994 and considerable renovation has taken place. There's an emphasis on sports, such as windsurfing, sailing and canoeing, as well as other games to keep people entertained. Divers are able to investigate nearby Banana Reef, with its superb scenery, mysterious caves and profusion of shark, barracuda and

Maldivian women are allowed more freedom than in many other traditional Islamic societies.

NORTH MALE ATOLL

bannerfish. As you might expect with Club Med, French as well as English is spoken here, and the clientele is predominantly young and international.

Full Moon

The resort is on Furana, an island with early Buddhist connections. Popular with couples, Full Moon has achieved a relaxed, get-away-from-it-all atmosphere, nevertheless a mere 7 km (4 miles) from the airport. All accommodation is luxury standard, in modern, two-storey blocks and "water bungalows", built on stilts over the ocean and a delight for those who like to be lulled to sleep by the gentle lapping of waves. The southern lagoon is good for snorkellers and there's also a fully equipped, air-conditioned gym, well-designed pool and two floodlit tennis courts.

Bandos

One of the Maldives' biggest diving centres, Bandos Island Resort has a first-rate PADI diving centre, a permanently staffed clinic and a decompression chamber. There's a sauna, gym, swimming pool, billiard room and squash court, and it's also child-friendly, with a baby-sitting service available. The choice of restaurants and large conference centre attract both business visitors and expats from Male, for whom a free ferry is provided on Thursday evening and Friday morning. With a capacity for 650 guests, Bandos won't seem quite like the deserted island of Maldivian myth, but then its main appeal is as a lively, sociable resort.

Kuda Bandos

If Bandos gets too sociable, however, this adjacent uninhabited island awaits. The government has prevented development here, and so the island retains its pristine beauty. On Fridays it's popular with workers from Male making the most of their day off.

Thulagiri

Circular Thulagiri is a small island about 5 km (3 miles) north of Bandos whose guests mainly hail from Germany, France, Switzerland and the UK. There's a conscious striving for the traditional look here. The thatched bungalows have *sataa* panelling (mats made from strips of dried screwpine) and are separated by bougainvillaea bushes. Sailing, windsurfing and waterskiing are all available and the food is rated highly. The *dhoni* ride from the airport takes about an hour.

Paradise Island

A bold attempt to trademark the all-important P-word, this is a resort on the grand scale. The size of narrow Lankanfinolhu has

NORTH MALE ATOLL

Trailing a veil of coral, the tiny resort of Giravaru was once occupied by people who claimed to be the original inhabitants of the Maldives.

been considerably increased by land reclamation. All of its rooms face the ocean, have satellite TV and are equipped with open-air showers. The over-water bungalows have sundecks looking out on a beautiful lagoon. The full complement of water sports is available, plus fishing expeditions, flood-lit tennis courts, squash, badminton, sauna and gym facilities, and a children's pool. The bar is open 24 hours a day and there are several restaurants, including Japanese (the resort receives many visitors from Japan), as well as a disco, live music and traditional cultural events.

Soneva Gili Resort and Spa
On Lankanfushi, northeast of Malé, this luxurious resort with 44 villas and residences is the first to be built entirely over water Some rooms can only be reached by private boat.

Tari Village
This tiny resort on Kanu Hura has a reputation for being laid-back—which is probably inevitable as it is one of the major surfing spots in the Maldives. Between April and November, surfers from as far as Australia arrive here for the swells at Pasta Point, known throughout the surfing world for its powerful left-handers.

Kuda Huraa Reef Resort

Recently redeveloped as a firmly upmarket, pricey resort, Kuda Huraa has more than 100 stylish and very luxurious villas, either by the beach or over the ocean. The restaurants and facilities are first-rate and transfers from the airport tend to dispense with *dhonis* in favour of a more jet-setting speedboat.

Kanifinolhu Resort

A tastefully designed resort with rooms in two-storey blocks and individual cottages, featuring plenty of traditional wooden latticework, beams and balustrades. You can take part in all the main watersports, there are plenty of excursions on offer, as well as a good child-minding service. Night-time entertainment includes a disco and frequent live music acts. One of the most prominent features is the large, shallow lagoon, which provides excellent sailing opportunities, and there's a wide beach.

Lohifushi

This island was first developed as a coconut plantation and still has groves that lend a splendidly tropical atmosphere to the place. The rooms are split into three levels of accommodation, from rustic coral bungalows to luxury air-conditioned suites with open-air bathrooms. The facilities include a volleyball court, children's playground and even a football pitch. The diving centre is fortunate to have a couple of first-rate sites nearby, such as the Aquarium, with its abundance of moray eels and white-tipped reef sharks.

SURFING SAFARI

Unlike California or Australia, the Maldives isn't generally known for its surfing culture, but among the cognoscenti it's a famous hotspot. The reason for its appearance on any surfer's map of the world is a conjunction of two things: the swells created by the southwest monsoon from May to November, and the geographical peculiarity of the atolls, where gaps in the surrounding outer reefs can cause powerful surf. The best breaks are in the North Male Atoll, which have been given names such as Honky's, Pasta Point, Cola's and Sultan's. They are all accessible from the Maldives' most renowned surfing resort, Tari Village. For those seeking new surf, though, it's possible to head out on a safari boat with a local guide who will take you to less crowded breaks—an unforgettable experience for even the most jaded surfing palate.

NORTH MALE ATOLL

Gasfinolhu

In the early days of Maldivian tourism this was a campsite—a backpacking type resort that's hard to imagine now anywhere in the Maldives. Gasfinolhu on Mahureva Island has since been completely revamped as an elegant resort that caters for the Italian market.

Meerufenfushi Island Resort

The most easterly island in the atoll, Meerufenfushi, meaning "freshwater island", was named by fishermen for the abundant reserves of rainwater that were found here. It's relatively large, with plenty of land given over to lush vegetation, including some fruit plantations, and as such can easily absorb more than 200 modern rooms. The pace is very relaxed, prices fairly low and the mainly European visitors young. There are the usual sports facilities plus a safari boat that heads out into the atoll for three-day excursions. The bonus for divers is a superb underwater cliff known as the Colosseum, and a truly fantastic display of exotic fish.

Helengeli

This is the most remote resort in the atoll. It's about 50 km (30 miles) north of Male airport, and a *dhoni* ride will take you 3$^{1}/_{2}$ hours, which can be either a very relaxing or very queasy experience, depending on the state of your sea-legs. The name compounds the sense of isolation— *helengeli* means "shaking island reef" as it faces the northeast monsoon head on, at which time the seas around here can get very choppy. The resort reopened in 1996 after extensive renovation. Snorkellers will delight in the long house reef, while the lack of any competition for the ocean around here means that dive sites, with several shipwrecks to choose from, are marvellously unspoilt.

Eriyadhu

On the northwest side of the atoll across from Helengeli, this is a delightful island washed by pristine waters. The rooms are of a basic economy standard, but they're nicely positioned along the beach, and the resort is renowned for its friendliness. The bar is especially attractive, opening out onto the ocean. There's a good beach and a fine house reef just offshore where snorkellers can see manta and eagle rays, tuna and reef fish. Guests are mostly from Germany. From this and the two following resorts, there is easy access to some of the best dive sites in the Maldives, including Kuda Faru with its beautiful coral and large groups of sharks.

NORTH MALE ATOLL

Makunudhoo

Makunudhoo Island, about 6 km (4 miles) to the south, is a luxury resort, with bungalows designed in traditional Maldivian style and using locally made materials. Island-hopping, snorkelling, night-fishing and even an introductory diving trip are often included in the price of the accommodation. There's also a beauty centre and masseurs to knead away your aches and pains.

Summer Island Village

Ziyaaraifushi is home to Summer Island Village, a resort which aims at promoting the simple things in life with prices to match. The clientele is largely German. The water is excellent for underwater photography. The house reef, called Blue Lagoon, has a constant gathering of pufferfish, banded trevally and triggerfish.

Reethi Rah Resort

Reethi Rah means "beautiful island". Also called Medhufinolhu, it's fish-shaped, a mere 80 m (87 yd) across, but 850 m (930 yd) in length, with the restaurant at one end, thatched cottages at the other, and an over-water café in between. The atmosphere is un-fussy and relaxed and the resort is

popular with British guests. It's also one of those independent-minded places that sets its clocks one hour ahead of the rest of the country, so that the guests can enjoy sunshine till 7 p.m.

Taj Coral Reef Resort

A recent facelift has taken the heart-shaped island of Hemba-dhoo upmarket. The resort has two score rooms, including over-water accommodation, and a range of watersports such as windsurfing, sailing and water-skiing. The close-fringing reef is guaranteed to please snorkellers.

Kudahithi

This is probably the most exclu-sive resort in the Maldives, with only seven bungalows. All are luxuriously fitted and individu-ally themed along the lines of Sheikh's Room, Safari Lodge, Captain's Cabin and so on. It's the only resort in the country without a diving centre, though guests can use the facilities on neighbouring Boduhithi, whose bungalows are generally filled with Italian holidaymakers.

Nakatchafushi

It may have once been the retreat of the sultan's powerful court as-trologer, the *Nakatchchaa*. The bungalows have sloping thatched roofs, and there are several res-taurants and an over-water bar.

Public transport, Maldivian style.
No traffic jams here.

NORTH MALE ATOLL

In the villages, coral walls around the gardens ensure privacy; the streets of coral sand are kept spotlessly clean.

At either end of the island is a tapering spit of sand, with a fine beach on the northern side.

Banyan Tree
The resort on Vabbinfaru Island offers 5-star luxury. The elegant ocean-facing villas with seashell-twirl roofs have marble bathrooms, king-size four-poster beds and private gardens. Windsurfing, snorkelling and use of the catamaran come with the room rate; night fishing and diving safaris are also available.

Ihuru
A small and perfectly formed circle of an island, Ihuru is owned and managed by a Maldivian firm, and both the decor and ambience reflect the country's easy-going charm. It's a mid-price resort with thatched bungalows, a dazzling turquoise lagoon and a house reef called The Wall that's famous for its stingray population.

Baros
One and a half hour's *dhoni* ride from Male, Baros is a stylish resort mostly frequented by British and German guests. Some of the palm-thatched bungalows are built over the water, and all have direct-dial phones (by no means universal in Maldivian resorts).

SOUTH MALE ATOLL

Apart from the usual sports facilities, you can take part in big game and night fishing.

Giravaru

Just 10 km (6 miles) west of Male, the resort has been recently upgraded but nonetheless maintains a low-key atmosphere. The Giravaru people who once lived on the island claimed they were the original inhabitants of the Maldives, and kept themselves separate from other Maldivians for centuries. Recent history hasn't been kind to them. Moved from their island to Hulhule because of erosion to Giravaru, they were again uprooted in 1968 when the airport was ready to open. They now live on the west side of Male, and their numbers are dwindling.

South Male Atoll

On the other side of Vaadhoo Kandu, a channel 500 m (1,640 ft) deep with extremely powerful currents, lies the South Male Atoll. Among its 30 islands, 17 are resorts and only 3 of the remainder are inhabited. The most populous of these is Guraidhoo, with around 550 people. It's a classic example of a Maldivian fishing village and was also the place where various sultans fled to escape rebellions and invasion attempts on Male. Today, Guraidhoo is a regular port of call for tourists from the surrounding resorts on day trips and has several souvenir shops.

Laguna Beach Resort

Visitors from all around Europe favour this extremely comfortable luxury resort located on Velassaru, just across the channel from Male. A full range of activities is available, including floodlit tennis court, plus several restaurants, a children's pool, and an on-call medical service.

Bolifushi

About 5 km (3 miles) southwest of Laguna Beach, this cosy little resort boasts good beaches and is popular with divers for the house reef, which has the wreck of a 9-m (29-ft) yacht. The boat has proved a great attraction for napoleon wrasse, white-tipped reef sharks and eagle rays.

Vadoo Diving Paradise

On the edge of Vaadhoo Kandu, Vaadhoo island has a long history. Archaeologists have found remains of a Buddhist temple that suggest the original inhabitants were here long before the Maldives' conversion to Islam. The resort receives a large proportion of visitors from Japan, who come for the excellent dive sites. The thatched over-water bungalows have glass coffee tables that let you see through to the fish below.

SOUTH MALE ATOLL

Taj Lagoon Resort
An Indian hotel chain owns this resort on Embudu Finolhu. The island is only 50 m (55 yd) wide, which explains why most of the rooms are built over the ocean. Embudu has a large and sandy lagoon that is excellent for watersports. A boat was sunk in shallow water here and it is perfect for first-time divers to practise on.

Embudu Village
Located on a small, pear-shaped island, not to be confused with its above-mentioned neighbour, the resort has over 100 inexpensive rooms nestling among a thick carpet of trees. The restaurant and bar are informal spots with open sides and sand floors. This is a great island for snorkellers, where the coral-covered house reef clings tightly to the shore, then drops dramatically some 20 m (65 ft) to the ocean bed.

Dhigufinolhu
This long, rectangular sand bar boasts good beaches and a large lagoon. The resort is comfortable and family-oriented, although it may feel a little crowded. However, there's a walkway linking it to Palm Tree Island, which gives access to some more space and better snorkelling areas as well. All the resort's unsightly necessities—generator, desalination plant, etc.—are tucked away on another island, also connected by a walkway.

Palm Tree Island and Boduhuraa
Palm Tree Island is a smaller and more expensive resort on Veliganduhuraa, with its own restaurant and a good outside reef with a snorkelling platform. More facilities are available by crossing over to Dhigufinolhu.

Boduhuraa is the third resort to be opened on the same reef. It's linked by walkway to Veliganduhuraa, and lends a certain expansiveness to these tiny islands.

Biyadhoo and Villi Varu
The management like to boast of two resorts for the price of one with these near neighbours. A free *dhoni* ferry service links the islands and you can charge food and drink to your room at both. Biyadhoo has superb diving facilities and a fine close-fringing reef. It is the only resort in the Maldives to have a hydroponic garden, providing fresh fruit and vegetables for the restaurant.

Villi Varu is a smaller island with more of an isolated feel to it. Both resorts are popular with British guests.

Cocoa Island Resort
The 30 stylish rooms and 6 villas of minute Makunufushi are delightfully designed to resemble

SOUTH MALE ATOLL

wooden *dhonis*, built out above the ocean. Apart from great diving, there's also a gym and spa, including yoga pavilion, meditation area and Ayurvedic treatments. Windsurfing, waterskiing and sailing come with the accommodation and there's a restaurant serving a blend of Indian and Sri Lankan cuisine. An interesting geographical feature of Makunufushi is its long sandbar.

Kandooma

An economy-price resort just a stone's throw from the inhabited Guraidhoo Island, it has decent rooms and a nice rustic-style restaurant, but its prime attraction is the proximity to some of South Male Atoll's best dive sites. The gigantic Kandooma Caves are spectacular, while the Kandooma Thila has superb coral and fish. Guraidhoo Kandu is a Protected Marine Area and a wonderland of exotic underwater life.

Fun Island Resort

The fun on long, thin Bodufinolhu comes from a combination of one disco, two restaurants and three bars. Would-be Robinson Crusoes can wade across to two uninhabited islands at low tide.

Olhuveli View

This attractive island is a favourite with Japanese tourists, and there's a good Japanese restau-

rant, a Japanese-managed diving school and, of course, a karaoke bar. All the luxury rooms have telephones and TVs and along with the usual range of sports you can enjoy a round of mini-golf.

Rihiveli Beach Resort

On Mahaana Elhi Hura, the southernmost of the atoll's islands, Rihiveli is a haven of luxury and tranquillity. Each room has a hammock on the terrace, the thatched restaurant is scenically located over the sea, and you can walk through the lagoon to uninhabited islands. The accommodation is expensive, but includes fishing, windsurfing and many other activities as well. At 44 km (24 miles) from the airport, transfers take an hour by speedboat.

Fiha Lhohi

The resort is marketed almost exclusively through German tour operators. It's very reasonably priced and has good facilities, both for sports during the day and socializing at night.

Rannalhi

Club Rannalhi is a comfortable mid-price resort with thatched-roof chalets and a pleasant atmosphere. The island has a good house reef, nice beaches and an impressive number of coconut palms imported from Addu Atoll in the south of the country.

OTHER RESORTS
Ari Atoll, Northern Atolls, Southern Atolls

Ari Atoll
Situated on the other side of a 40-km (25-mile) channel west of South Male Atoll, Ari is the third of the Maldives' main triumvirate of resort areas. Along with the smaller adjacent Rasdhoo Atoll, Ari comes under the adminstrative region of Alifu. The capital is Mahibadhoo, a major fishing island. Thoddoo, to the north of Rasdhoo Atoll, is known for its 17th-century mosque, ruined Buddhist temple and watermelon crop. Quarries on Maamigili and Fenfushi supply the nation's coral and sand for building.

A latecomer to the tourist business, this region is rapidly developing. It takes some time and effort to get here after you've landed at Male Airport, but the journey gives an outstanding view of the Maldives' breathtaking atoll formation.

Veligandu
One of only two resorts in Rasdhoo Atoll, Veligandu favours a simple, rustic appearance. Most of the public areas have sand floors, while open-air bathrooms give the rooms a suitably back-to-

Ari is one of the most popular atolls for diving trips.

nature feel. The resort is 50 km (30 miles) from Male and guests normally arrive by seaplane.

Kuramathi
This was once an inhabited island, and several pre-Islamic era Buddhist relics have been found, some of which are now in the National Museum in Male. By 1970, the population had fallen to a mere 124 and was resettled onto Rasdhoo. Kuramathi is one of the few islands in the Maldives to have more than one resort—in fact there are three. It's a place where you can really get away from the crowd and head off into a tropical wilderness—or at least to a different resort's restaurant. There is also a six-person decompression chamber here.

Kuramathi Village is made up of round thatched cottages and a couple of good restaurants, plus a *dhoni* that's been transformed into the bar. There are over-water bungalows at the luxury Cottage Club, while at the other end of the island, Blue Lagoon is an attractive resort with thatched bungalows surrounded by flowers.

Gangehi
A small resort at the top end of the market, Gangehi caters mainly for Italian guests. The island is 39

ARI ATOLL

a delight, with mangroves, palms and various exotic flowers.

Velidhu Island Resort
Some 68 km (42 miles) from the airport, it takes two hours to reach the resort even by speedboat. The island has a sheltered lagoon and is especially popular with Italian and Swiss visitors.

Nika Hotel
Famously stylish and expensive, Nika is a superb resort of cavernous villas, designed in rustic materials of coral stone, thatched roofs and local timber, and shaped like seashells. Each villa has a private garden and its own slice of beach. The cuisine is first-rate and, to set the seal on its difference, the resort's clocks are two hours ahead of Male, making the daylight stretch till 8 p.m.

Madoogali
This resort was opened in 1988 by the same team that runs Nika

Hotel, and it shows. Though mid-price, it's a classy, beautifully landscaped island with individual coral stone bungalows. Virtually all the bookings are made through an Italian operator.

Fesdhu
Fesdhu Fun Island lives up to its name with a relaxed atmosphere and essentially laisser-faire attitude to its international mix of guests. The cottages are in traditional thatched style. Fesdhu's house reef is well-known for its precipitous 20-m (65-ft) drop, its hard coral and intriguing sea creatures such as stonefish, octopus and lionfish. A maximum of two guests a day plus picnic can head off by *dhoni* to Gaathafushi, a genuinely deserted dot of an island a short distance away.

Moofushi
A picturesque little island whose resort offers all-in packages predominantly to Italian tourists. The

4 THE FOUR BEST OCEAN SIGHTS Manta rays flying elegantly through the water are an unforgettable sight. Famous for its **turtles**, the Maldives can boast five of the world's seven different species. The 15-m **whale shark** is the largest known fish and guaranteed to send a chill up any spine. Remarkable **wrasse** come in all shapes and sizes from the 20-cm banded wrasse to 2-m napoleons—in some species the female can change sex if there's a shortage of males.

ARI ATOLL

nearby Moofushi Kandu channel has some dramatic overhangs cut out of the reef and is packed with fish. The channel itself is patrolled by sharks and rays.

Athurugau

Coral stone and dark wood in the restaurant and other public areas characterize Athurugau Island Resort. The modern-style rooms are linked by covered walkway. Athurugau's guests come mainly from Britain and the continent on a full-board basis.

Thundufushi

Aimed at very much the same market as Athurugau, this resort has the same number and type of rooms and also offers full-board, though here, exceptionally, that also includes cigarettes. Non-smokers beware.

Angauga

A wide international mix of guests head for Angaga Island Resort, attracted by its reputation as a perfect place for chilling out. Each very comfortable thatched bungalow is equipped with an *undhoali*, a Maldivian swing-seat, outside. The restaurant has an especially impressive thatched dome roof.

The resort is 100 km (60 miles) from the airport and people tend to arrive either by speedboat or seaplane.

Mirihi

This tiny island—a mere 300 by 260 m (328 by 284 yd)—is almost swamped by the resort, and the majority of rooms are of necessity built over water. Nevertheless, its compactness seems to appeal to the mainly German clientele who enjoy the convivial atmosphere.

Maldives Hilton

Students of globalization will be interested to discover that even the Maldives now boasts a Hilton. The hotel opened on Rangali Finolhu in 1997. There are 100 well-equipped bungalows, with 30 over-water bungalows on a small adjacent island and connected by footbridge to the main resort. The facilities are excellent and the island is blessed with fine beaches. Look out for the glistening coral on the reef, for which the island is famous.

Sun Island

The new kid on the atoll, Sun Island was ready for guests in 1998. It's a large resort on Nalaguraidhoo, one of the Maldives' bigger islands and has a wide range of watersports, restaurant and bar facilities.

Holiday Island

An older sibling to the above-mentioned Sun, Holiday Island, as the promoters call Dhiffushi,

ARI ATOLL

has modern, luxury beach-front rooms, each with satellite TV and telephone. It's more than 100 km (60 miles) from Male and the transfer here is by speedboat or seaplane. The resort is very close to Maamigili, an interesting inhabited island with a fishing village and 17th-century mosque.

Ari Beach

A pioneer of the low-price, "no shoes, no news" style of Maldivian resort, Ari Beach has inexpensive, no-frills accommodation, good-value food and drink, and long, sandy beaches. It attracts an informal younger crowd, including singles and independent travellers, generally a rare breed in the Maldives.

Kuda Rah

Another small luxury resort, with modern rooms packed onto a Lilliputian-sized island. The guests here are drawn mainly from the Italian market.

Vakarufalhi

This new resort looks attractive, with traditional-style thatched *cabanas* emerging scenically from the coconut palms. Inside, all the mod-cons are on tap. Plenty of trips are available for island-hopping around this part of the atoll. Both this and Kuda Rah are well-placed for diving trips to the exceptional Dhigurashu

Kandu area, where fantastic caves have luxuriant growths of seawhips, black coral bushes and sea fans, and vast schools of big-nose unicornfish and yellow-back fusiliers amaze the onlooker.

Machchafushi

The room rates and bar prices are not the only attractions at this economically priced resort. Accommodation is in marble-floored bungalows with thatch covering the metal roofs, and over-water rooms. The restaurant is supplied from the island's own vegetable garden and there's a wide, shallow lagoon for water-sports.

Twin Island

So-called because it has a neighbouring almost identical island, Twin Island is a luxury-standard resort of blue roofs, boisterous animators (high-energy people employed to keep the guests entertained) and superb Italian cuisine. The resort, on Maafushivaru Island, is used solely by Italians.

Ranveli Beach

Located on Viligilivaru, an island on the eastern edge of the atoll, the resort caters mostly for Italian guests. The diving around the island is good, with lots of exotic fish in the area and interesting coral and caves in the Dhangethi

ARI ATOLL

Kandu channel. Dhangethi, an inhabited fishing island, is very close and has a huge banyan tree in the middle which is said to be 200 years old.

Vilamendhoo
The resort's modern-style chalets have palm thatch on the roofs in a nod towards the rustic look, but their main appeal is air-conditioned comfort. The restaurant serves both western and oriental cuisine, and all the usual watersports facilities are to be found. At each end of this thickly wooded island is a picturesque sandbank, and there's excellent snorkelling and diving.

Lily Beach
Long and narrow, Huvahendhoo Island lacks the tropical palm-covered appearance of most Maldivian islands, but makes up for it with dazzling white-sand beaches and a house reef that closely borders the island, providing marvellous snorkelling. The resort has comfortable beachfront rooms and over-water bungalows.

Ellaidhoo
The rooms on the island are basic standard, but the guests here are usually more concerned with the remarkable diving opportunities than the level of accommodation. Ellaidhoo has possibly the best house reef in the Maldives, a 750-m (820-yd) wall with hard and soft coral, large caves and a catalogue of Maldivian marine life, including oriental sweetlip, blue-face angelfish, moorish idol and many others. Qualified divers have unrestricted access to the reef. The guests are mostly from Germany, but the island's reputation is enough to ensure that diving enthusiasts from elsewhere come here too.

Halaveli
Another Italian-dominated resort, where a clock in reception shows the time in Italy as well as on the island. The lagoon is good for windsurfing and sailing, and out on the reef the Halaveli Wreck is a noted dive site where stingrays live and turtles visit.

Bathala
Bathala, an attractive little island with round thatched cottages and a pleasantly rustic atmosphere, is another superbly located place for divers. The fringing house reef plunges to 30 m (98 ft) and has plenty to interest even experienced divers, while several other exciting dive sites, including the lively Bathalaa and Maagaa Kandu channels, are within easy access.

Maayafushi
Half-moon shaped and with a wide lagoon, Maayafushi is a

resort with a lived-in feel to it. It's mid-priced and most guests are full-boarders from Germany. The Maaya Thila, 4 km (2.5 miles) northwest of the island, has a huge concentration of white-tip reef sharks as well as several other reef fish, and many impressive caves and coral outcrops.

Northern Atolls

The northern atolls are mostly well beyond the tourist zone, although there are several interesting inhabited islands which with some effort and an inter-atoll permit you could visit. Utheemu, in the northernmost atoll of North Thiladhunmathee, is the birthplace of Mohamed Thakurufaanu, and his house and a memorial centre can be seen. Narudhoo, in North Miladhunmadulu Atoll, is extremely picturesque, enhanced by its inland lakes. Alifushi, in Raa Atoll, is the home of Maldivian *dhoni* building, while Thulhaadhoo, in Baa Atoll, is famous for the production of red, black and yellow lacquerware.

Baa and Raa are the next atolls up from Ari Atoll; east of these is Lhaviyani. Tourism is expanding rapidly in this region.

Baa Atoll

Sonevafushi is an expensive, up-market resort on Kunfunadhoo Island, about 115 km (70 miles) from Male, but only a short way from the atoll capital, Eydhafushi. The island is relatively long, densely wooded and with a feeling of tropical wilderness. The villas are all luxurious—even equipped with CD players—and the restaurant is excellent.

New resorts have opened on other islands: the Coco Palm Resort on Dhunikolhu; the Italian-managed Club Valtur on Kihaadhuffaru; the Reethi Beach Resort on Fonimagoodhoo, with a great house reef; and Royal Island (with Ayurvedic spa) on Horubadhoo, which has screwpine trees, white-tailed tropic birds and the ruins of an old mosque.

Raa Atoll

The only resort in this atoll is Pearl or Meedhupparu Island, 40 minutes by seaplane from Male. It is ringed by a wide beach; the house reef is 70 m (76 yd) away; there's an ayurvedic centre, a dive base and watersports centre.

Lhaviyani Atoll

Kuredu Island Resort was the first in this atoll. Inexpensive, it has two restaurants, bars, good sports facilities and the chance to go off for a 24-hour stint on a deserted island. The resort is very popular with divers, who can explore the marvellous Kuredu Caves and house reef, and the exhilarating Kuredu Express channel nearby.

Northern Atolls • Southern Atolls

Vilamendhoo offers plenty of shade and a perfect beach.

Four newer resorts in the atoll are Palm Beach Island, with a superb beach and a lagoon in which it's possible to find manta rays; Komandhoo, a small island with a close-fringing reef; Kanuhuru Beach and Spa Resort, and Hudhufushi, unusually shaped like a wishbone (two islands that have joined together over time), with fantastic beaches and a shallow lagoon that attracts stingrays and baby sharks.

Southern Atolls

In the entire chain of southern atolls, resorts are few and far between—one of them being on Gan, across the equator and accessible only by plane. It is very difficult to travel outside these restricted tourist zones, which is unfortunate as the atolls here contain some of the most fascinating archaeological sites in the Maldives. Nilandhoo, in North Nilandhoo Atoll, boasts the superb Aasaari Mosque, as well as a profusion of ruins and artefacts dating from long before the Islamic era. Many islands, such as Isdhoo, Gamu and Kodey, have fine examples of ancient mounds, or *hawittas*, which were excavated by H.C.P. Bell in the 1920s and Thor Heyerdahl in the 1980s. Bell thought they dated from the pre-Islamic Buddhist age, while

Heyerdahl argued they were built by an even earlier mysterious aboriginal people, the Redin.

North and South Nilandhoo

In the past few years three new resorts have developed in these atolls some 80 km (50 miles) southwest of Male: Filitheyo Island in North Nilandhoo; Velavaru (or Turtle Island) and Vilu Reef on Meedhuffushi Island in South Nilandhoo. Vilu Reef has round thatched villas, good facilities, a spectacular lagoon and a house reef that's a mere pebble's throw from the beach. All these resorts give access to interesting inhabited islands such as Nilandhoo and Dharabhoodoo, famous for the turtles that use the beach for laying their eggs.

Felidhoo Atoll

Alimathaa Aquatic Resort tells you immediately where its heart lies. The guests, who are mostly German, come here to enjoy excellent diving and snorkelling on the house reef. It's an attractive resort, with 102 rooms built in rustic design.

Dhiggiri Tourist Resort, about 7 km north of Alimathaa, prides itself on its simple accommodation and natural setting. The island is nicely located for Manta Point, where manta rays gather during the southwest monsoon.

Mulaku Atoll

Two new resorts have been built in this atoll south of Felidhoo: Medhufushi Island Resort, with thatched roof villas scattered over

5 THE FIVE BEST DIVE SITES With several excellent sites to choose from, we recommend the following: **Fotteyo**, in the Felidhoo Atoll, with its coral-covered caves and numerous exotic fish is considered by many to be the best in the Maldives; the **Halaveli Wreck**, in North Ari Atoll, is a cargo ship that's home to famously friendly stingrays; in Faadhippolhu Atoll, the **Kuredu Express** isn't a train ride, but a beautiful steep outside reef crowded with grey reef sharks, napoleon wrasse and large schools of trevally; the **Shipyard**, in the same atoll, has two sunken vessels to explore; **Fushifaru Thila** is a Protected Marine Area of luxuriant soft coral, stunning reef fish and strong currents.

SOUTHERN ATOLLS

the island or on stilts over the water; and Hakura Club on Hakuraahuraa, with a desert island atmosphere. They are well poised to take advantage of the unspoilt waters in this area. The Mulaku Kandu channel is especially noted for its outer reef that plummets 100 m (328 ft), and its brilliant range of fish.

Addu Atoll

Equator Village (or Ocean Reef Club), on Gan Island, situated less than half a degree south of the equator, is the only resort in this southernmost atoll and it's a world apart from anywhere else in the entire country. It shares the island with a large airport runway, built originally by the British and abandoned in 1976. Now, scheduled Air Maldives planes arrive once a day—and the flight from Male over the southern atolls is one of the most spectacular you'll ever experience.

The resort itself has been established on the site of the old RAF base, and although the pleasant air-conditioned rooms are in new buildings, they retain the layout and appearance of the former barracks. In many ways, though, the hotel's military history only adds to its character; the attractive pink and white open-sided restaurant is in the former sergeants' mess, and the bar has an ancient billiard table inherited from the British. The Equator Village has a small beach and a swimming pool, with a good house reef for diving, while further up the coast the wreck of the *British Loyalty*, an oil tanker sunk by a Japanese torpedo in 1942, provides a major point of interest for divers and fish alike. Near the hotel is a War Memorial, in honour of those troops of the British Indian Army who died here—mainly from illness rather than in action—during World War II.

What is unique about staying on Gan, however, is the chance to enjoy unrestricted access to inhabited islands. Gan is linked to three fishing islands by a string of British-built causeways, and you do not require a permit to visit them (although you must not stay after dark). You can rent a bike and cycle to Feydhoo, Maradhoo and the atoll capital, Hithadhoo, along a 16-km (10-mile) road that's the longest in the Maldives. The villages are formed in a typically Maldivian grid-pattern, with low-level houses made from coral stone, a main mosque, and shops that cater to the local community rather than the tourist market. Even better, you can go to small tea houses, sample typical Maldivian cuisine and enjoy traditional Maldivian hospitality at its best. In the villages, the local people tend to hide away in the shade of their courtyards.

47

CORAL WORLD

Only a small number of animals capable of tunneling or crawling, such as molluscs and worms, can adapt to life in the shifting sands. The coral reef, on the other hand, makes an ideal home for thousands of sea creatures that can hide away in the caves, cling to the ridges and use the colours to camouflage themselves.

The reef is not rock but a living substance, the skeletons of countless millions of tiny marine organisms—coral polyps. It has taken some 25 million years to build the thousands of reefs comprising the Maldives. They are continually under construction as each dead polyp adds its minute skeleton to an underwater architecture of Gothic simplicity and striking beauty. Resembling tiny flowers, the polyps bloom on the surface of polyparies, which in turn form shapes resembling antlers, organ pipes, fans or delicate shrubs, in various shades of red, blue and brown. In full expansion, the reefs can grow several centimetres a year.

The minute polyps are very hard to please. Only when the conditions are just right—when the sea is clear, bursting with oxygen, warm and not too deep—do they take the plunge. The average water temperature has to be between about 22 and 28°C, with plenty of sunshine. Just one degree more spells danger to the coral, seriously threatened by global warming which causes bleaching on the upper surface.

The polyps reproduce by laying eggs, once a year. In late spring or early summer, soon after a full moon, the females release bundles of eggs which float to the surface, while practically simultaneously the males release sperm. Each fertilized egg produces a coral larva, barely a millimetre in length. It sinks to the bottom a few days later to search for a good spot to start a new coral colony. The growing polyp feeds on, and in turn feeds, microscopic algae. It develops a multitude of buds which all develop into new polyps. The structure grows in all directions, in forms and colours specific to each variety.

A coral colony, no matter how large, cannot form a reef on its own. This is why each reef is so beautiful and so unique, made up of several species that have spread gradually over the substructure created by the preceding generations. In the Maldives, more than 70 varieties of coral comprise the millions of living colonies.

Cultural Notes

Dhoni

This graceful boat is to the Maldives what the double-decker bus is to London—an essential means of transport, but also a symbol and much-photographed tourist sight. It's likely that the *dhoni* is a version of the Arabian *dhow*, although the *dhoni* has been adapted to the special needs of sailing around the reefs, lagoons and ocean swells of the Maldives. Its most distinctive feature is the curving prow, which is nowadays detachable as it prevents easy access at modern jetties. The boats are hand-built by craftsmen known as *kissaru wadin*, who are ranked in the higher echelons of Maldivian society (the name means "curved carpenters"). A team of 12 workers can knock a *dhoni* out in about two months, using timber from coconut palm for the hull and imported lighter wood for buoyancy on top. The whole structure is fitted together with wooden pegs and copper nails, and the hull coated with fish oil.

With a broad beam that can take prodigious amounts of fish, cargo or passengers, the *dhoni* has proved a great success. A redesigned model rolled out of the government's Alifushi workshop in 1985. *Dhoni* skippers turned up their noses at it. Its flatter, more extended bow was an object of derision and the boats had to be sold off cheaply. The designers have had the last laugh, though. The new boats are now recognized as more efficient and the Alifushi yard can no longer meet the demand.

Fanditha

The ancient myths of the Maldives have long been frowned upon by the Islamic theologians, but they have proved highly resilient. Maldivians have shown a marked ability to juggle the unorthodox with their more mainstream faith. There is still a strong belief in the existence of *jinni*, invisible supernatural beings who intervene in people's lives, often for harmful ends. If some misfortune occurs — such as an unsuccessful fishing expedition or trouble within a marriage—a Maldivian may take comfort in readings from the Koran, but to be doubly sure will consult a *fanditha* man. Part magician, part scientist, the *fanditha* man is a highly respected member of the community and possesses an arcane knowledge of potions and charms specifically designed to defeat recalcitrant *jinni*. Some

CULTURAL NOTES

may dismiss it as mere superstition, but in a country where the dangers of the ocean dominate everyday life to such an extent, Maldivians simply want as many insurance policies as possible.

Islam

The cement that holds the thousand islands of the nation together, Islam is at the heart of Maldivian culture. Every inhabited island—including Hulhule, the airport island—has a mosque and the capital contains more than 20. The branch of Islam practised here is Sunni, as opposed to Shi'ite, and all children study the teachings of Islam from an early age. Men and women attend separate mosques and no other religions are allowed—indeed, objects of worship from other faiths may well be retained at customs until departure. However, the Maldivian version of Islam can also be very liberal. Maldivian women are not forced to wear the veil and have equal access to education, employment and property rights. And Maldivian judges interpret the Islamic *shari'a* law in surprisingly lenient ways—typically, serious criminals face banishment to one of the country's many remote islands rather than execution. For Maldivians, this isn't as idyllic as it might seem to Westerners. It means separation from family and a very public sense of shame. But it seems to work. There are very few second offenders, and crime rates in the Maldives are miniscule.

Mohamed Thakurufaanu

The most famous name in Maldivian history is regularly encountered by tourists due to the amount of roads and buildings named after him. Born on the island of Utheemu in the early 16th century, he was the second son of the local chief. During the years of Portuguese rule, he and his two brothers, Ali and Hassan, became exponents of the hit-and-run guerrilla tactic, using fast boats and classic Maldivian navigational skills to attack the Portuguese in Male and flee before there was any response. His masterminding of the eventual triumph over the Portuguese in 1573 earned him the sultanate, which he consolidated by marrying the previous sultan's daughter. Also famed for the many reforms he brought in to Maldivian society—which included the introduction of coinage instead of cowrie shells—Thakurufaanu died a national hero in 1585. His wooden house, on the island of Utheemu in the north of the Maldives, has been restored and a museum built. More accessible, his modest tomb is in the grounds of the small Bihuroazu Kamanaa mosque in the centre of Male.

Shopping

For the best variety and value you have to head for the capital. All the shopping hot spots are conveniently situated within a few minutes' walk of the jetty where boats land from the resorts.

Where?

Behind the Presidential Palace, the area known as the Singapore Bazaar, bordered by Orchid, Chandani and Fareedhee streets, is packed with souvenir shops and probably has the best prices in town, helped by the willingness of shopkeepers to haggle. Be sure to check out prices at a few stores before making a purchase, and be aware that the ones the tour guides recommend might not be the cheapest. On Orchid Magu, the State Trading Organisation occupies a modern-looking building and has a well-stocked supermarket. Lastly, the Duty Free at Male offers very good prices on electrical goods, tobacco and cosmetics.

What?

A lot of the goods on sale will be standard souvenir paraphernalia imported from elsewhere. For more interesting gifts, look out for the following products "made in the Maldives".

There are some fine local handicrafts, in particular the traditional lacquered wooden boxes, bowls and vases, strikingly designed in brightly coloured patterns.

Attractive and uniquely Maldivian mats, made from either reeds or coconut leaves and coir (the fibrous material from the outside of coconut shells), are handwoven by craftsmen and women out on the islands.

Maldivian jewellery—necklaces, rings and bracelets—are fashioned from local materials such as mother-of-pearl.

In a different vein, but still showing a typically exuberant taste for colour, Maldivian postage stamps are always very bright and popular with collectors. And T-shirts printed in Male, usually covered in brilliantly coloured tropical fish, are an unmistakable declaration of your feelings towards the island nation.

More unusual—and bulky— mementoes include the *gudu-gudu*, a Maldivian hookah which you will see people smoking out on the islands, and a *bodu beru*, the traditional drum.

Sports

On Sea...

Swimming is good almost everywhere and the scuba diving and snorkelling excellent. Surfers will find superb waves during the southwest monsoon period from spring to November. A surfing trip takes a lot more planning here than in most countries, however, and it's wise to check out a specialist travel agent. Windsurfers can be rented and lessons taken at most resorts. You can also learn to sail, although it's an expensive sport to become addicted to. The boats used are catamarans. Water-skiing and parasailing are available at some resorts.

The Maldives boasts some of the world's best fishing. Big game fishing takes place year round; the main species including blue and black marlin, barracuda, yellowfin tuna, wahoo, jackfish, sailfish, sharks and dorado.

A popular pursuit is night fishing. Bigger on atmosphere than thrills, it concentrates on the reef fish that live nearer to the resorts. Groupers, snappers and squirrel fish are among those which might take the bait.

Canoes can be rented by the hour at several resorts. The shallow lagoons are good for beginners in particular. Generally, it is not permissible to go out onto the ocean in a canoe.

...and on Land

Many of the resorts have tennis courts and racquets and balls can be hired. The luckier ones are floodlit. For the real keep-fit fanatics, some of the top-notch resorts have well-appointed gyms where you can have a full workout in air-conditioned comfort.

Maldivian Sports

Bashi is an ancient Maldivian game played by girls. Its name would seem to describe perfectly what happens to the ball, as it is whacked back and forth across a net by two teams of 11 facing away from each other. In fact, *bashi* is Dhivehi for the palm leaf implement once used as a bat. It has been replaced nowadays by a tennis racquet.

Maldivian boys favour football and cricket. Impromptu matches can be seen on any available patch of ground around Male. More serious matches are held at the National Stadium on Majeedi Magu. There's a Maldivian football league, with three divisions, and cricket tournaments take place in the stadium as well.

Dining Out

The islanders like their food spicy, but considerate resort chefs may well dampen things down for palates less used to red-hot chillis. If you want to try it the Maldivian way, head for a Male tea shop.

Breakfast

Most resorts offer a standard buffet breakfast. The islanders might start the day, on the other hand, with *mas huni*: smoked tuna mixed with onions, grated coconut, chilli and lime juice, and served with *roshi*, unleavened bread.

Short Eats

Tea houses look quite dark and slightly off-putting from outside, and they are the preserve of Maldivian men. Visitors shouldn't let that deter them, for inside they are clean and sociable places. They specialize in tasty snacks called short eats (or *hedhikaa* in Dhivehi). A range of these will be put in front of the customer, who will be charged afterwards for anything consumed.

On the table you will find *bajiyaa*, samosa-shaped pastries stuffed with tuna, onions, ginger and lemongrass; *kulhi boakibaa*, a square fishcake flavoured with chilli, ginger and coconut; *gulha*, fried spicy fish balls; and *theluli kavaabu*, a deep-fried fish rissole. Sweets include *bondi*, a finger-shaped coconut stick, and *huni folhi*, a fried *roshi* filled with a coconut and honey paste.

Long Eats

More substantial meals are *garudiya*, the quintessential Maldivian fish soup served with rice and spicy side dishes of chilli, lime and onions; and *hanaakurimas*, a dry fish curry that can be boosted with *rihaakuru*, a pungent tuna paste sometimes spread on warm *roshis*.

Resort Cuisine

In the ritzier resorts there might be a choice of restaurants and they will offer international style cooking—from Italian to Thai—that is also international in standard. Other resorts, offering full or half board from a main kitchen, tend to be more limited in scope and stick to what can be fairly institutional three-course dinners. This is often the result of being further away from the vari-

DINING OUT

Tonight's dinner arriving in Male harbour.

ety of products that can be bought near the capital. If it's a major concern, be sure to check the type of restaurants at the resort you are considering staying at.

Fruit
The atolls are not overflowing in exotic fruit. The soil simply isn't rich enough. There are lots of coconuts, though, and tasty little bananas grow down in Addu Atoll, for instance. Demand from the resorts has lead to an increase in cultivation wherever it is possible, and these days you might be lucky enough to get a Maldivian papaya, watermelon or mango for dessert.

Drinks
Alcoholic drinks are forbidden to Maldivian citizens but in the resorts, imported beer, wine, spirits and cocktails are on sale, though very pricey.

Coca-Cola is made locally with desalinated water, as are bitter lemon and soda water. Non-alcoholic beer is widely available. *Suji* is a rich sweet drink concocted from semolina, coconut milk, sultanas, nuts and spices. The indispensible Maldivian drink, however, is *raa*, a toddy tapped from the palm tree by a specialist called a *raa veri*. It's very sweet and delicious, but with a powerful aroma.

The Hard Facts

Airports

All flights from overseas arrive at Male International Airport, located on its own island a short distance from the capital. Visitors on pre-booked holidays often take charter flights direct from their own country, whereas scheduled departures go via the carrier's hub airport.

The terminal at Male has a bank where you can change money, but it's unlikely you will need very much local currency as payment for all facilities can be added to your hotel bill. There is also a snack-bar, tourist shop, information office and, when you have gone through customs on departure, fairly extensive duty-free facilities. Before leaving the Maldives you will have to pay a departure tax in US dollars.

Also operating from Male International Airport are internal Air Maldives flights to a handful of local airports, although Gan in Addu Atoll is the only one that foreigners can fly to without an inter-atoll permit. Helicopter flights have been discontinued.

The most inaccessible resorts are best reached by air taxi. Two companies operating seaplanes are based at the airport: Maldivian Air Taxi (MAT) and Trans Maldivian Airways (TMA). They "land" on the lagoon nearest to the resort island, to be met by *dhonis* that take you to shore—about as dramatic an entrance as you are ever likely to make. Certainly, any flight across the Maldives is guaranteed to be a spectacular and highly memorable experience.

Climate

Straddling the equator, the Maldives is one of those countries where the idea of seasons is meaningless. Temperatures vary little throughout the year, ranging between 25.4°C (78°F) and 30.4°C (87°F). On average, there are more than 2,500 hours of sunshine annually, tempered by very pleasant breezes off the ocean. There's certainly no need to take any more clothing than lightweight cottonwear, sandals, a hat and a pair of sunglasses.

The annual rainfall is approximately 2000 mm (78 in) and, being typically tropical, it can rain at any time. This is why you will find that ominous umbrella sitting in your hotel wardrobe. The year is divided into two monsoon periods, a southwest monsoon from May to November, and a northeast one from Decem-

THE HARD FACTS

ber to April, which are the drier months and the peak season for tourism. But the showers only last for a matter of minutes, after which the sun shines as brightly as ever.

Communications

The main post office is in Male, on Chandani Magu, opening daily, except Friday, 7.30 a.m.– 6 p.m. On the resort islands, stamps are available at the resort shop, and postcards and letters can generally be posted in the reception area.

The Maldives telecom company is called Dhiraagu. International direct dialling using a phonecard and reverse-charge calls can be made from many public boxes. Cards cost 30, 50, 100, 200 and 500 Rf. Calls aren't cheap; a 100 Rf card buys a 2-minute chat to Europe. It's less expensive to phone between midnight and 8 a.m. The Dhiraagu office in Male is next to Sultan's Park on Medhuziyaarai Magu. Fax facilities are available here and at the main hotels and resorts.

The country code for the Maldives if you are calling from abroad is 960. There are no area codes.

To dial overseas from the Maldives, dial 00 and the country code (the US is 1, the UK is 44), then the area code (minus the initial 0) and the local number.

To call the operator dial 110. International directory enquiries is 190.

Crime

Most criminal cases in the Maldivian courts involve citizens who have been caught drinking alcohol or engaging in forbidden extra-marital pursuits. Petty theft is a problem, but almost never affects foreigners. For Western visitors the Maldives feels like a refreshingly crime-free society. You can walk the streets of Male without any worry over personal safety, other than the need to dodge speeding motorbikes, and your belongings will be safe in your room. Nevertheless, it's always wise not to tempt fate. Most resorts have a safe, where you may feel happier about leaving your passport, jewellery and travellers cheques. Keep wallets and handbags concealed if you leave them on the beach while you go for a swim.

Customs

You are allowed to bring sufficient quantities of cigarettes, tobacco or cigars for personal use.

It is illegal to import alcohol, drugs, pornographic material (which can be interpreted quite widely by the authorities), pork, firearms or idols for worship.

There's a government ban on the export of black coral and all 57

▶ THE HARD FACTS

products related to the killing of turtles, such as carvings made from their shells.

Diving

It's estimated that almost two-thirds of all visitors to the Maldives go diving at some point during their stay. They are understandably attracted by the clear water, the stunning array of colourful fish, extravagant coral promoted by the strong Indian Ocean currents, and an armada of old shipwrecks to hunt around. The main diving season is from August to April, with the best visibility in the first four months of the year.

First-time divers need to pass an introductory course, but almost every resort has a diving centre whose instructors hold internationally recognized teaching certificates such as the PADI. A diving qualification validated by these centres will be valid throughout the world. Qualified divers should remember to bring their driving-test certificates and log book with them.

All the equipment, such as the tank, weight belt and computer, can be hired from the resort dive schools, though if you intend to do a lot of diving it might be worth investing in a snorkel, mask and fins, which can also be used separately for snorkelling, and will guarantee a good fit.

Strictly speaking, everyone who wants to dive should have a diving medical certificate, but in practice you will be asked to sign a medical statement form declaring your fitness to dive. People with health problems such as recurring dizziness, asthma or diabetes should consult a doctor. It's best to arrange for this before you leave home (although there are suitably qualified doctors at the AMDC clinic and ADK Hospital in Male and at the Bandos Island Medical Centre). Contact your local dive shop or club to find out the nearest doctor who specializes in this.

It's worth taking out extra travel insurance that specifically covers diving—it's an extremely well regulated and safe sport in the Maldives, but if something does go wrong, the specialized treatment needed will be very expensive. Again, ask at a dive shop or club about the best insurance policies available. The Divers Alert Network (DAN) is particularly known among divers for its expertise in arranging diving insurance.

Even the most tentative beginner will need to become familiar with the divers' code of practice. The key to modern diving is conservation and careful management of the marine environment. The Maldives government is acutely aware of the need to safe-

THE HARD FACTS

guard its greatest natural resource and has created 15 Protected Marine Areas aimed at preserving the quality of dive sites. These areas are intended to restrict the damage caused by overfishing, coral mining, dumping of rubbish and use of anchors. Divers can do their bit by observing the rules—no touching or kicking the coral, no feeding, handling or chasing the fish or any other animals such as turtles, and above all no littering. If you are out on a diving safari, be especially sure to collect any rubbish harmful to the environment, such as plastic materials and batteries, and take it away with you.

Treated with the right care and respect by all concerned, the Maldives' marvellous underwater world will be around for many future generations to enjoy.

Emergencies

Most problems can be dealt with at the hotel reception. Emergency telephone numbers in Male are:

Police: 119

Ambulance: 102

Fire: 118.

There are no foreign embassies or high commissions in the Maldives, only consular agents, who are based in Male and work part-time. They should be contacted only for serious situations such as a lost passport or worse, and *not* for lost plane tickets or money.

Formalities

You will need a valid passport, but no visas are required prior to entry into the Maldives. Visitors are given a 30-day tourist visa on arrival. Anyone arriving from regions infected with yellow fever must show an inoculation certificate.

All visitors without a hotel reservation should be in possession of US$30 per day of their intended stay. Note: the Entry Card which you fill in before arrival requires that you have an address in the Maldives. If you are an independent traveller, it's worth having a reservation for at least the first night at one of the hotels in Male, otherwise you will be held up unnecessarily at passport control until accommodation is found.

Health

The Maldives have remarkably few of the health problems suffered by other countries in the region. The resorts in particular are scrupulously clean places, with high standards of hygiene in rooms and restaurants—you will even see the beaches being meticulously checked for litter each morning.

It's probably best to stick to bottled mineral water, although the local tap variety is mainly desalinated sea water and unlikely to cause any harm. There are mosquitoes but no malaria, so there's no need to take the unpleasant preventative tablets, and there's little in the way of dangerous wildlife on the islands.

Most health problems arise from the things visitors specifically go to the Maldives to enjoy. Top of the list is too much exposure to the sun. Remember, you are almost on the equator and the sun is extremely powerful here. Wear a hat, use a good sun-screen and keep in the shade as much as possible, especially in the middle of the day. Always wear a T-shirt when snorkelling for any length of time as the sea won't prevent the sun from burning your back. Drink plenty of mineral water to avoid dehydration.

The sea presents its own set of dangers. If you go diving, be aware of decompression sickness, known colloquially as "the bends". This is caused by surfacing too quickly from the deep, and is recognized by symptoms of dizziness, extreme tiredness, pains in the limbs, spasmodic coughing and breathlessness. There are decompression chambers on Bandos Island and Kuramathi.

Also bear in mind that coral is extremely sharp. Certain fish, such as stonefish and butterfly fish, are poisonous to touch, and many will bite if you try to feed them.

Holidays and Festivals

Many of the Maldives' public holidays are based on the Islamic lunar calendar and are therefore moveable. The most important festival is Ramadan, held on the ninth month of the Islamic year.

Martyr's Day, held at the beginning of Ramadan, commemorates the death of Sultan Ali VI in the struggle against the Portuguese in 1558.

Kuda Eid celebrates the end of Ramadan.

Al'h'aa Eid is the Prophet Mohammed's birthday

National Day celebrates the ousting of the Portuguese from Male in 1578

Huravee Day recalls the expulsion of the Malabars after their attack on Male in 1752.

Fixed public holidays are:

January 1	New Year
July 26	Independence Day (the end of the British Protectorate)
November 3	Victory Day (celebrating the defeat of Tamil mercenaries who attempted a coup in 1988)
Nov. 11–12	Republic Day (the foundation of the second republic in 1968)
10 December	Fisheries Day

THE HARD FACTS

Languages

The language spoken in the Maldives is Dhivehi, unique to the country, whose name, *Dhivehi Raajje*, means "island kingdom". To outsiders, the script appears as a bewildering series of dots and squiggles, and when it is transliterated into Latin characters, the names, streets and buildings end up with any number of different spellings. No one seems to care about consistency. The sound "doo", for instance, may also be written *du, dhu* or *dhoo*. Fortunately, English is widely spoken.

Here are a few words and phrases for those who want to attempt speaking Divehi:

Hello/goodbye	*a-salam alekum*
How are you?	*haalu kihine?*
Fine	*vara gada*
Yes/no	*aa/noo*
Thank you	*shukuria*
All right, OK	*enge*
How much is this?	*mi kihavaraka?*
cheap	*agu heyo*
expensive	*agu bodu*
now	*mihaaru*
today	*miadu*
tonight	*mire*
tomorrow	*madamma*
yesterday	*iye*
morning	*hendhunu*
afternoon	*mendhuru fas*
good	*barabah*
enough	*heo*
island	*dhu*
large island	*fushi*
small island	*finolhu*
large	*bodu*
small	*kuda*

And some numbers:

1	*eke*	2	*de*
3	*tine*	4	*hatare*
5	*fahe*	6	*haie*
7	*hate*	8	*ashe*
9	*nue*	10	*diha*
11	*egaara*	12	*baara*
13	*tera*	14	*saada*
15	*fanara*	16	*sorla*
17	*satara*	18	*ashara*
19	*onavihi*	20	*vihi*
30	*tiris*	40	*saalis*
50	*fansaas*	60	*fasdolaas*
70	*hai-diha*	80	*a-diha*
90	*nua-diha*	100	*sateka*

Media

The *International Herald Tribune* finds its way into a few of the resorts, while at some of the better bookshops in Male you will be able to pick up new editions of *Time* and *Newsweek*. The major national daily newspapers, *Aafathis* and *Haveeru*, usually have a couple of pages in English.

Few of the resorts have TV sets in the rooms, and addicts will have to battle over the channels in a TV lounge. Satellite channels such as CNN and BBC World are generally available. The local broadcaster, TV Maldives, has a 20-minute bulletin in English each night at 9 p.m.

61

THE HARD FACTS

With a short-wave radio, you can listen to the BBC World Service or Voice of America. The frequencies change at different times of the day.

Money
The unit of currency in the Maldives is the Rufiyaa (Rf), which is divided into 100 laari (L). Coins range from 1 to 50 laari, and 1 and 2 rufiyaa; banknotes from 5 to 500 rufiyaa. US dollars are equally acceptable. In fact you will not need much Maldivian currency as the resorts and the larger hotels in Male take the main credit cards and charge in US dollars. On the resort islands, you can sign for meals, drinks, day trips, gifts from the shop and hire of diving equipment and pay by credit card at the end of your stay, making a Maldivian resort a virtually cashless society.

Opening Hours
The following times are a general guide. Hours tend to vary, especially during Ramadan.

Banks open Sunday to Thursday 8 a.m.–1.30 p.m.

Most *shops* open any time between 6 and 9 a.m. (though later on Friday) and can close as late as 9–11 p.m.

Restaurants serve at lunchtime and evenings, while *cafés* and *tea houses* will be open all day and close late at night.

Photography
Respect the "No Photography" signs. Never take pictures inside a mosque or of worshippers at prayer. Out on the islands, ask permission before taking someone's photo.

Public Transport
Going anywhere within the Maldives usually involves a boat trip. The basic craft, the *dhoni,* mainly plies its trade as a taxi between the airport, Male and the nearer resorts. They can be hired for single trips or by the day, but with a speed of around 10 kph, they are unlikely to take you very far.

For longer distances you can travel in jetset-style by seaplane taxi. If you want to fly south of the equator to Gan you can book onto a scheduled Air Maldives flight.

More down-to-earth taxis operate in Male. It is small enough to walk around, but in the midday sun an air-conditioned cab to take you back to your hotel might seem like a very good idea.

Social Customs
The Maldives is that rare place where tourists are still popular among the locals. They know that foreigners bring in much needed cash, but there is also a genuine interest in where their visitors come from and how they are enjoying the Maldives' abundant

THE HARD FACTS

delights. Perhaps this positive encounter is due to the fact that tourists are largely kept to their own resort islands. It is also because most foreigners respect the social customs of the Maldives, which are founded on centuries of Islamic practice.

Although dress is resolutely informal and the branch of Islam here fairly liberal, there are some codes of behaviour which should be carefully observed. Alcohol is available on the resort islands and banned elsewhere, and shouldn't be taken on day trips to Male or the inhabited islands. When visiting the capital, people should be covered from shoulder to knee— T-shirts and Bermuda shorts will do—and women should not wear see-through clothing. Beachwear should be confined to the resorts. Nude bathing is forbidden, and carries a fine of US$1000.

Time
The Maldives follow GMT +5 all year round. The sun rises every morning around 6 a.m. and sets about 6 p.m. Some resorts alter their clocks so that night falls later.

Tipping
Restaurants in Male and some resorts authomatically add a 10% service charge to all your bills and, as the government discourages tipping, you are not obliged to give anything. However, it's customary to leave a small gratuity for the room cleaner, your regular waiter and the porter, especially if you stay at a resort for a week or more.

Toilets
There are public toilets in Male, but you might prefer to head either for the large STO building on Orchid Magu, which has toilets on every level, or else the larger hotels, most of which are away from the shopping area at the east side of the island.

Tourist Information Offices
The airport has a tourist information counter, although it's not always brimming with brochures and leaflets. The Ministry of Tourism has an office along the waterfront in Male near to the Nasandhura Palace Hotel.

Voltage
Electric current is from 220 to 240V. Sockets are mainly for three square-pin plugs. Bathrooms in the resort rooms tend to be equipped with multi-use sockets for razors, etc. Electricity in most of the resorts comes from their own generators, which are tucked away in discreet corners of the island. They guarantee a supply 24 hours per day, something which several of the inhabited islands don't enjoy.

INDEX

Addu Atoll 47
Angauga 41
Ari Beach 42
Athurugau 41
Baa Atoll 44
Bandos 28
Banyan Tree 34
Baros 34–35
Bathala 43
Biyadhoo 36
Boduhuraa 36
Bolifushi 35
Cocoa Island 36
Coral 49
Dhigufinolhu 36
Dhoonidhoo 23
Ellaidhoo 43
Embudu Village 36
Eriyadhu 31
Farukolhufushi 27–28
Felidhoo Atoll 46
Fesdhu 40
Fiha Lhohi 37
Full Moon 28
Fun Island 37
Funadhoo 23
Gan 45, 47
Gangehi 39–40
Gasfinolhu 30
Giravaru 35
Halaveli 43
Helengeli 31
Holiday Island 41–42
Hulhule 22
Ihuru 34
Kandooma 37
Kanifinolhu 30
Kuda Bandos 28
Kuda Huraa Reef 30
Kuda Rah 42
Kudahithi 33
Kuramathi 39
Kurumba Village 27
Laguna Beach 35

Lhaviyani Atoll 44–45
Lily Beach 43
Lohifushi 30
Maayafushi 43–44
Machchafushi 42
Madoogali 40
Makunudhoo 33
Maldives Hilton 41
Male 15–22
Meerufenfushi 31
Mirihi 41
Moofushi 40–41
Mulaku 46–47
Nakatchafushi 33–34
Nika Hotel 40
Nilandhoo 45–46
Olhuveli View 37
Palm Tree Island 36
Paradise Island 28–29
Raa Atoll 44
Rannalhi 37
Ranveli Beach 42–43
Reethi Rah 33
Rihiveli Beach 37
Soneva Gili Resort and Spa 29
Summer Island Village 33
Sun Island 41
Taj Coral Reef 33
Taj Lagoon 36
Tari Village 29
Thulagiri 28
Thundufishi 41
Twin Island 42
Vadoo Diving Paradise 35
Vakarufalhi 42
Velidhu Island 40
Veligandu 39
Vilamendhoo 43
Viligili 23
Villi Varu 36

GENERAL EDITOR
Barbara Ender-Jones
EDITOR
Ann Wood
LAYOUT
Luc Malherbe
PHOTO CREDITS
Bernard Joliat:
pp. 11, 23, 29, 45;
Imagefrance.com/Giulio:
pp. 5, 32;
Rives/VISA: pp. 14, 26;
Kobeh/BIOS: pp. 24–25, 48;
Volkmar E. Janicke: p. 34;
Imagefrance.com/Frances:
pp. 1, 38
MAPS
JPM Publications

Copyright © 2005, 1999
by JPM Publications S.A.
12, avenue William-Fraisse,
1006 Lausanne, Switzerland
E-mail:
information@jpmguides.com
Web site:
http://www.jpmguides.com/

All rights reserved. No part of this book may be reproduced or transmitted in any form or by any means, electronic or mechanical, including photocopying, recording or by any information storage and retrieval system without permission in writing from the publisher.

Every care has been taken to verify the information in the guide, but neither the publisher nor his client can accept responsibility for any errors that may have occurred. If you spot an inaccuracy or a serious omission, please let us know.

Printed in Switzerland
Weber/Bienne (CTP) — 04/10/01
Edition 2005

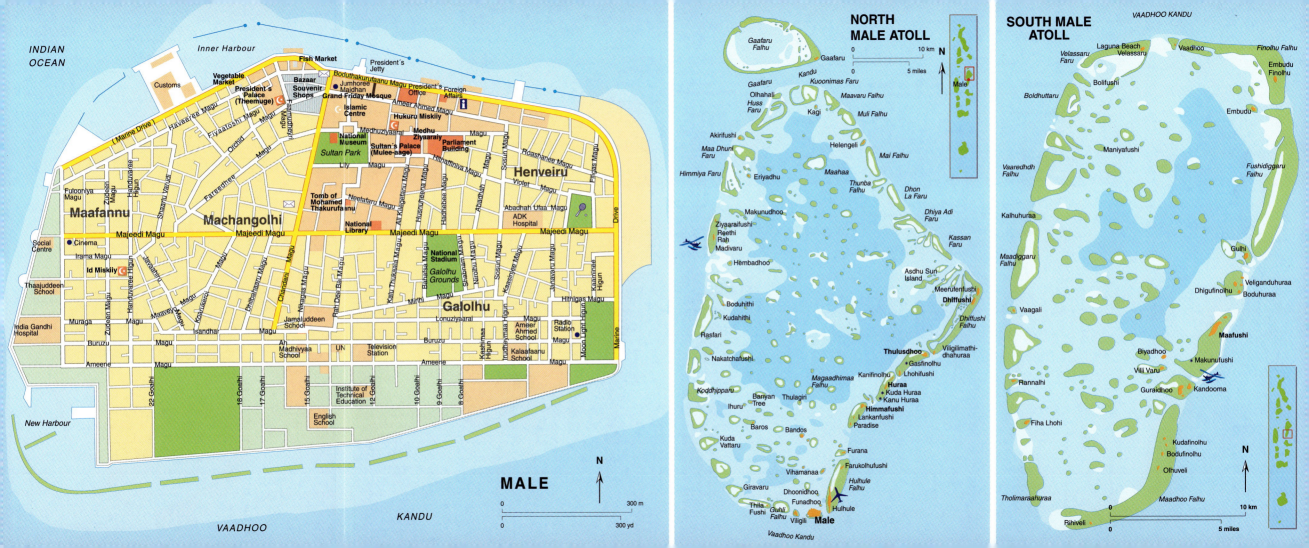

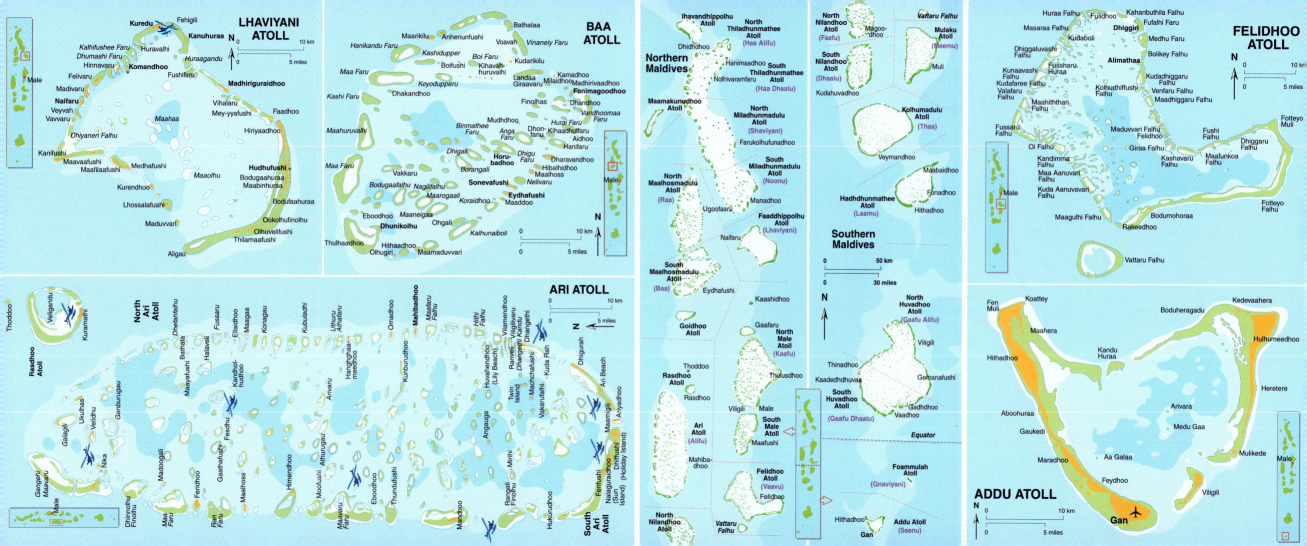